Hymns of the New Testament

Hymns of the New Testament

Lyrics by Isaac Watts

Music by J.L. Smith

Cover Art Work by Emily Schultz

White Stone Press

Anchorage

2010

To Bob and Frieda

A New Song to the Lamb that was Slain

Rev. 5:6-12

Isaac Watts

J.L.Smith

Behold the glories of the Lamb
Amidst his Father's throne;
Prepare new honors for his name,
And songs before unknown.

Let elders worship at his feet,
The church adore around,
With vials full of odors sweet,
And harps of sweeter sound.

Those are the prayers of the saints,
And these the hymns they raise,
Jesus is kind to our Complaints,
He loves to hear our praise.

[Eternal Father, who shall look
Into thy secret will?
Who but the Son shall take that book,
And open every sea]?

He shall fulfil thy great decrees,
The Son deserves it well:
Lo! in his hand the sovereign keys
Of heav'n, and death, and hell!]

Now to the Lamb that once was slain
Be endless blessings paid;
Salvation, glory, joy, remain
For ever on thy head.

Thou hast redeemed our souls with blood,
Hast set the pris'ners free;
Hast made us kings and priests to God,
And we shall reign with thee.

The worlds of nature and of grace
Are put beneath thy power;
Then shorten these delaying days,
And bring the promised hour.

The Deity and Humanity of Christ

John 1:1,3,14; Col. 1:16

Isaac Watts

J.L. Smith

Ere the blue heav'ns were stretched abroad,
From everlasting was the Word:
With God he was; the Word was God,
And must divinely be adored.

By his own power were all things made;
By him supported all things stand;
He is the whole creation's head,
And angels fly at his command.

Ere sin was born, or Satan fell,
He led the host of morning stars:
Thy generation who can tell,
Or count the numbers of thy years?

But lo! he leaves those heav'nly forms,
The Word descends and dwells in clay,
That he may hold converse with worms
Dressed in such feeble flesh as they.

Mortals with joy beheld his face,
Th' eternal Father's only Son;
How full of truth! how full of grace!
When through his eyes the Godhead shone.

Archangels leave their high abode
To learn new mysteries here, and tell
The loves of our descending God,
The glories of Immanuel.

The Nativity of Christ
Luke 1:30ff; 2:10ff

Isaac Watts
J.L. Smith

Behold, the grace appears!
The promise is fulfilled;
Mary, the wondrous virgin, bears,
And Jesus is the child

[The Lord, the highest God,
Calls him his only Son;
He bids him rule the land abroad,
And gives him David's throne.]

To bring the glorious news
A heav'nly form appears;
He tells the shephards of their joys,
And banishes their tears.

"Go humble swains," said he,
"To David's city fly;
The promised infant born to-day
Doth in a manger lie."

[In worship so divine,
Let saints employ their tongues;
With the celestial host we join,
And loud repeat their songs:

"Glory to God on high!
And heav'nly peace on earth;
Goodwill to men, to angels joy,
At our redeemer's birth."]

Salvation's Born Today

Luke 2:10-20

Isaac Watts

J.L.Smith

"Shepherds, rejoice! lift up your eyes,
And send your fears away;
News from the regions of the skies,
Salvation's born to-day.

Jesus, the God whom angels fear,
Comes down to dwell with you;
Today he makes his entrance here,
But not as monarchs do.

No gold nor purple swaddling bands.
Nor royal shining things;
A manger for his Cradle stands,
And holds the King of kings.

Go, shepherds, where the infant lies,
And see his humble throne
With tears of joy in all your eyes,
Go, shepherds, kiss the Son."

Thus Gabriel sang, and straight around
The heav'nly armies throng;
They tune their harps to lofty sound,
And thus conclude the song:

"Glory to God that reigns above!
Let peace surround the earth!
Mortals shall know their Maker's love,
At their Redeemer's birth."

Lord, and shall angels have their songs,
And men no tunes to raise?
O may we lose our useless tongues
When they forget to praise.

Glory to God that reigns above,
That pitied us forlorn;
We join to sing our Maker's love,
For there's a Savior born.

The Inward Witness to Christianity

1 Jn. 5:10

Isaac Watts

J.L.Smith

Questions and doubts be heard no more,
Let Christ and joy be all our theme;
His Spirit seals his gospel sure,
To every soul that trusts in him.

Jesus, thy witness speaks within;
The mercy which thy words reveal
Refines the heart from sense and sin,
And stamps its own celestial seal.

'Tis God's inimitable hand
That molds and forms the heart anew;
Blasphemers can no more withstand,
But bow, and own thy doctrine true.

The guilty wretch that trusts thy blood
Finds peace and pardon at the cross;
The sinful soul, averse to God,
Believes and loves his Maker's laws.

Learning and wit may cease their strife,
When miracles with glory shine;
The voice that calls the dead to life
Must be almighty and divine.

The Blessedness of Gospel Times

Mt. 13:16,17; Isa. 52:2,7-10

Isaac Watts

J.L.Smith

How beauteous are their feet
Who stand on Zion's hill!
Who bring salvation on their tongues,
And words of peace reveal!

How charming is their voice!
How sweet the tidings are!
"Zion, behold thy Savior King;
He reigns and triumphs here."

How happy are our ears
That hear this joyful sound,
Which kings and prophets waited for,
And sought, but never found!

How blessed are our eyes
That see this heav'nly light
Prophets and kings desired it long,
But died without the sight.

The watchmen join their voice,
And tuneful notes employ;
Jerusalem breaks forth in songs,
And deserts learn the joy.

The Lord makes bare his arm
Through all the earth abroad;
Let every nation now behold
Their Savior and their God!

The Humble Enlightened, and Carnal Reason Humbled

Luke 10:21-22

Isaac Watts

J.L. Smith

There was an hour when Christ rejoiced
And spoke his joy in words of prayer;
"Father, I thank thee, mighty God,
Lord of the earth, and heav'ns and seas.

I thank thy sovereign power and love
That crowns my doctrine and success,
And makes the babes in knowledge learn
The heights, and breaths, and lengths
   of grace.

But all this glory lies concealed
From men of prudence and of wit;
The prince of darkness blinds their eyes,
And their own pride resists the light.

Father, 'tis thus, because thy will
Choose and ordained it should be so;
'Tis thy delight t' abase the proud,
And lay the haughty scorner low.

There's none can know the Father right
But thoses who learn if from the Son;
Nor can the Son be well recieved
But where the Father makes him known."

Then let our souls adore our God,
Who deals his graces as he pleases;
Nor gives to mortals an account
Or of his actions or decrees.

Free Grace Revealed in Christ

Luke 10:21

Isaac Watts

J.L. Smith

Jesus, the man of constant grief,
A mourner all his days;
His spirit once rejoiced aloud,
And tuned his joy to praise:

"Father, I thank thy wondrous love,
That hath revealed thy Son
To men unlearned, and to babes
Has made thy Gospel known.

The mysteries of redeeming grace
Are hidden from the wise,
While pride and carnal reasonings join
To swell and blind their eyes."

Thus doth the Lord of heav'n and earth
His great decrees fulfil,
And orders all his works of grace
By his own sovereign will.

The Triumph of Faith

Rom. 8:33ff

Isaac Watts

J.L. Smith

Who shall the Lord's elect condemn?
'Tis God that justifies their souls;
And mercy, like a mighty stream,
O'er all their sins divinely rolls.

Who shall adjudge the saints to hell?
'Tis Christ that suffered in their stead;
And, the salvation to fulfil,
Behold him rising from the dead!

He lives! he lives and sits above,
For ever interceding there:
Who shall divide us from his love?
Or what should tempt us to despair?

Shall persecution, or distress,
Famine, or sword, or nakedness?
He that hath loved us bears us through,
And makes us more than conquerors too.

Faith hath an overcoming power;
It triumphs in the dying hour:
Christ is our life, our joy, our hope,
Nor can we sink with such a prop.

Not all that men on earth can do,
Nor powers on high, nor powers below,
Shall cause his mercy to remove,
Or wean our hearts from Christ our love.

Our Own Weakness and Christ Our Strength

2 Cor. 12:7,9,10

Isaac Watts

J.L.Smith

Let me but hear my Savior say,
"Strength shall be equal to thy day,"
Then I rejoice in deep distress,
Leaning on all-sufficient grace.

I glory in infirmity,
That Christ's own power may rest on me:
When I am weak, then am I strong,
Grace is my shield, and Christ my song.

I can do all things, or can bear
All suff'rings, if my Lord be there;
Sweet pleasures mingle with the pains,
While his left hand my head sustains

But if the Lord be once withdrawn,
And we attempt the work alone,
When new temptations spring and rise,
We find how great our weakness is.

[So Samson, when his hair was lost,
Met the Philistines to his cost;
Shook his vain limbs with sad surprise,
Made feeble fight, and lost his eyes.]

Hosannah to Christ

Matt. 21:9, Luke 19:38,40

Isaac Watts

J.L. Smith

Hosannah to the royal Son
Of David's ancient line!
His natures two, his person one,
Mysterious and divine.

The root of David here, we find,
And offspring is the same:
Eternity and time are joined
In our Immanuel's name.

Blest he that comes to wretched men
With peaceful news from heav'n!
Hosannah's of the highest strain
To Christ the Lord be giv'n!

Let mortals ne'er refuse to take
Th' hosannah on their tongues,
Lest rocks and stones should rise and break
Their silence into songs.

Victory Over Death

1 Cor. 15:55ff

Isaac Watts   J.L. Smith

O for an overcoming faith
To cheer my dying hours;
To triumph o'er the monster Death,
And all his frightful powers!

Joyful with all the strength I have
My quiv'ring lips should sing-
Where is thy boasted vict'ry, Grave?
And where the monster's sting?

If sin be pardoned, I'm secure,
Death hath no sting beside;
The law gives sin its damning power;
But Christ, my ransom, died.

Now to the God of victory
Immortal thanks be paid,
Who makes us conquerors while we die,
Through Christ our living head.

Blessed are the Dead that Die in the Lord

Rev. 14:13

Isaac Watts

J.L.Smith

Hear what the voice from heav'n proclaims,
For all the pious dead;
Sweet is the savor of their names,
And soft their sleeping bed.

They die in Jesus, and are blest;
How kind their slumbers are!
From suff'rings and from sins released,
And freed from every snare.

Far from this world of toil and strife,
They're present with the Lord;
The labors of their mortal life
End in a large reward.

A Vision of the Kingdom
of Christ among Men

Rev. 21:1-4

Isaac Watts

J.L.Smith

Lo! what a glorious sight appears
To our believing eyes!
The earth and sea are passed away,
And the old rolling skies.

From the third heav'n, where God resides,
That holy, happy place,
The new Jerusalem comes down,
Adorned with shining grace.

Attending angels shout for joy,
And the bright armies sing-
"Mortals, behold the sacred seat
Of your descending King.

"The God of glory down to men
Removes his blest abode;
Men, the dear objects of his grace,
And he the loving God.

"His own soft hand shall wipe the tears
From every weeping eye,
And pains, and groans, and griefs, and fears,
And death itself, shall die."

How long, dear Savior! O how long
Shall this bright hour delay?
Fly swifter round, ye wheels of time,
And bring the welcome day.

The Song of Simeon

Luke 2:27-32

Isaac Watts

J.L.Smith

Lord, at thy temple we appear,
As happy Simeon came,
And hope to meet our Savior here;
O make our joys the same!

With what divine and vast delight
The good old man was filled,
When fondly in his withered arms
He clasped the holy child!

"Now I can leave this world," he cried,
"Behold, thy servant dies;
I've seen thy great salvation, Lord,
And close my peaceful eyes.

This is the light prepared to shine
Upon the Gentile lands,
Thine Isr'el's glory, and their hope
To break their slavish bands."

[Jesus! the vision of thy face
Hath overpowering charms;
Scarce shall I feel death's cold embrace,
If Christ be in my arms.

Then while ye hear my heart-strings break,
How sweet my minutes roll!
A mortal paleness on my cheek,
And glory in my soul.]

Christ the Eternal Life

Rom 9:5

Isaac Watts

J.L. Smith

Jesus, our Savior and our God,
Arrayed in majesty and blood,
Thou art our life; our souls in thee
Possess a full felicity.

All our immortal hopes are laid
In thee, our surety and our head;
Thy cross, thy cradle, and thy throne,
Are big with glories yet unknown.

Let atheists scoff, and Jews blaspheme
Th' eternal life and Jesus' name;
A word of thy almighty breath
Dooms the rebellious world to death.

But let my soul for ever lie
Beneath the blessings of thine eye;
'Tis heav'n on earth, 'tis heav'n above,
To see thy face and taste thy love.

Flesh and Spirit

Rom. 8:1

Isaac Watts

J.L. Smith

What vain desires and passions vain
Attend this mortal clay!
Oft have they pierced my soul with pain,
And drawn my heart astray.

How have I wandered from my God!
And, following sin and shame,
In this vile world of flesh and blood
Defiled my nobler frame!

For ever blessed be thy grace
That formed my soul anew,
And made it of a heav'n-born race,
Thy glory to pursue.

My spirit holds perpetual war,
And wrestles and complains;
But views the happy moment near
That shall dissolve its chains.

Cheerful in death I close my eyes
To part with every lust;
And charge my flesh, whene'er it rise,
To leave them in the dust.

My purer spirit shall not fear
To put this body on;
Its tempting powers no more are there,
Its lusts and passions gone!

The Sight of God and Christ in Heaven

2 Cor. 5:8

Isaac Watts   J.L.Smith

Descend from heav'n, immortal Dove,	Adoring saints around him stand,
Stoop down and take us on thy wings,	And thrones and powers before him fall;
And mount and bear us far above	The God shines gracious through the man,
The reach of these inferior things:	And sheds sweet glories on them all.
Beyond, beyond this lower sky,	O what amazing joys they feel
Up where eternal ages roll;	While to their golden harps they sing,
Where solid pleasures never die,	And sit on every heav'nly hill,
And fruits immortal feast the soul.	And spread the triumphs of their King!
O for a sight, a pleasing sight	When shall the day, dear Lord, appear,
Of our Almighty Father's throne!	That I shall mount to dwell above,
There sits our Savior crowned with light,	And stand and bow amongst them there
Clothed in a body like our own.	And view thy face, and sing, and love?

A Hopeful Youth Falling Short of Heaven

Mark 10:21

Isaac Watts

J.L. Smith

Must all the charms of nature, then,
So hopeless to salvation prove?
Can hell demand, can heav'n condemn,
The man whom Jesus deigns to love?

The man who sought the ways of truth,
Paid friends and neighbors all their due;
A modest, sober, lovely youth,
And thought he wanted nothing new.

But mark the change; thus spake the Lord,
"Come, part with earth for heav'n today:"
The youth, astonished at the word,
In silent sadness went his way.

Poor virtues that he boasted so,
This test unable to endure;
Let Christ, and grace, and glory go,
To make his land and money sure!

Ah, foolish choice of treasures here!
Ah, fatal love of tempting gold!
Must this base world be bought so dear?
Are life and heav'n so cheaply sold?

In vain the charms of nature shine,
If this vile passion govern me:
Transform my soul, O love divine!
And make me part with all for thee.

A Vision of the Lamb
Rev. 5:6-9

Isaac Watts   J.L.Smith

All mortal vanities, begone,
Nor tempt my eyes, nor tire my ears;
Behold, amidst th' eternal throne,
A vision of the Lamb appears.

[Glory his fleecy robe adorns,
Marked with the bloody death he bore;
Seven are his eyes, and seven his horns,
To speak his wisdom and his power.

Lo! he receives a sealed book
From him that sits upon the throne;
Jesus, my Lord, prevails to look
On dark decrees and things unknown.]

All the assembling saints around
Fall worshipping before the Lamb,
And in new songs of gospel sound
Address their honors to his name.

Our voices join the heav'nly strain,
And with transporting pleasure sing,
"Worthy the Lamb that once was slain,
To be our Teacher and our King!"

His words of prophecy reveal
Eternal counsels, deep designs;
His grace and vengeance shall fulfil
The peaceful and the dreadful lines.

Thou hast redeemed our souls from hell
With thine invaluable blood;
And wretches that did once rebel
Are now made fav'rites of their God.

Worthy for ever is the Lord,
That died for treasons not his own,
By every tongue to be adored,
And dwell upon his Father's throne!

Hope of Heaven by the Resurrection of Christ

1 Pet. 1:3-5

Isaac Watts

J.L. Smith

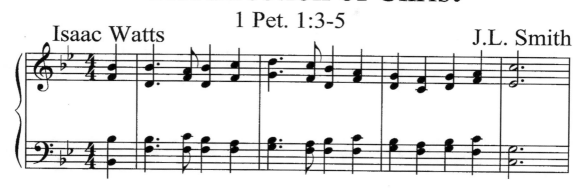

Blest be the everlasting God,
The Father of our Lord;
Be his abounding mercy praised,
His majesty adored.

When from the dead he raised his Son,
And called him to the sky,
He gave our souls a lively hope
That they should never die.

What though our inbred sins require
Our flesh to see the dust,
Yet as the Lord our Savior rose,
So all his followers must.

There's an inheritance divine
Reserved against that day;
'Tis uncorrupted, undefiled,
And cannot waste away.

Saints by the power of God are kept
Till the salvation come;
We walk by faith as strangers here,
Till Christ shall call us home.

Assurance of Heaven

2 Tim. 4:6,8,18

Isaac Watts

J.L.Smith

[Death may dissolve my body now,
And bear my spirit home;
Why do my minutes move so slow,
Nor my salvation come?

With heav'nly weapons I have fought
The battles of the Lord;
Finished my course, and kept the faith,
And wait the sure reward.]

God has laid up in heav'n for me
A crown which cannot fade;
The righteous Judge at that great day
Shall place it on my head.

Nor hath the King of grace decreed
This prize for me alone;
But all that love and long to see
Th' appearance of his Son.

Jesus the Lord shall guard me safe
From every ill design;
And to his heav'nly kingdom keep
This feeble soul of mine.

God is my everlasting aid,
And hell shall rage in vain;
To him be highest glory paid
And endless praise--Amen.

The Christian's Hidden Life

Col. 3:3

Isaac Watts   J.L. Smith

O happy soul that lives on high
While men lie grov'lling here
His hopes are fixed above the sky,
And faith forbids his fear.

His conscience knows no secret stings,
While peace and joy combine
To form a life whose holy springs
Are hidden and divine.

He waits in secret on his God,
His God in secret sees;
Let earth be all in arms abroad,
He dwells in heav'nly peace.

His pleasures rise from things unseen,
Beyond this world and time;
Where neither eyes nor ears have been,
Nor thoughts of sinners climb.

He wants no pomp nor royal throne
To raise his figure here;
Content and pleased to live unknown,
Till Christ, his life, appear.

He looks to heav'n's eternal hill
To meet that glorious day;
But patient waits his Savior's will
To fetch his soul away.

The Gospel:
The Power of God to Salvation
Rom. 1:16

Isaac Watts

J.L. Smith

What shall the dying sinner do
That seeks relief for all his woe?
Where shall the guilty conscience find
Ease for the torment of the mind?

How shall we get our crimes forgiv'n?
Or form our natures fit for heav'n?
Can souls all o'er defiled with sin
Make their own powers and passions clean?

In vain we search, in vain we try,
Till Jesus brings his gospel nigh;
'Tis there such power and glory dwell
As save rebellious souls from hell.

This is the pillar of our hope
That bears our fainting spirits up:
We read the grace, we trust the word,
And find salvation in the Lord.

Let men or angels dig the mines,
Where nature's golden treasure shines;
Brought near the doctrine of the cross,
All nature's gold appears but dross.

Should vile blasphemers with disdain
Pronounce the truths of Jesus vain,
I'll meet the scandal and the shame,
And sing and triumph in his name.

None Excluded from Hope

Rom. 1:16; 1 Cor. 1:24

Isaac Watts

J.L.Smith

Jesus, thy blessings are not few,
Nor is thy gospel weak;
Thy grace can melt the stubborn Jew,
And bow th' aspiring Greek.

Wide as the reach of Satan's rage
Doth thy salvation flow;
'Tis not confined to sex or age,
The lofty or the low.

While grace is offered to the prince,
The poor may take their share;
No mortal has a just pretence
To perish in despair

Be wise, ye men of strength and wit,
Nor boast your native powers;
But to his sovereign grace submit,
And glory shall be yours.

Come, all ye vilest sinners, come,
He'll form your souls anew;
His gospel and his heart have room
For rebels such as you.

His doctrine is almighty love;
There's virtue in his name
To turn the raven to a dove,
The lion to a lamb.

Truth and Sincerity

Phil. 4:8

Isaac Watts

J.L.Smith

Let those who bear the Christian name
Their holy vows fulfil;
The saints, the followers of the Lamb,
Are men of honor still.

True to the solemn oaths they take,
Though to their hurt they swear;
Constant and just to all they speak,
For God and angels hear.

Still with their lips their hearts agree,
Nor flatt'ring words devise;
They know the God of truth can see
Through every false disguise.

They hate th' appearance of a lie
In all the shapes it wears;
They live in truth, and when they die,
Eternal life is theirs.

While hypocrites and liars fly
Before the Judge's frown,
His faithful friends, who fear a lie,
Receive th' immortal crown.

Faith the Way to Salvation

Rom. 1:16; Eph. 2:8,9

Isaac Watts

J.L.Smith

Not by the laws of innocence
Can Adam's sons arrive at heav'n;
New works can give us no pretence
To have our ancient sins forgiv'n.

Not the best deeds that we have done
Can make a wounded conscience whole;
Faith is the grace, and faith alone,
That flies to Christ, and saves the soul.

Lord, I believe thy heav'nly word,
Fain would I have my soul renewed;
I mourn for sin, and trust the Lord
To have it pardoned and subdued.

O may thy grace its power display,
Let guilt and death no longer reign;
Save me in thine appointed way,
Nor let my humble faith be vain.

A Lovely Carriage

Matt. 10:16

Isaac Watts

J.L. Smith

O 'tis a lovely thing to see
A man of prudent heart,
Whose thoughts, and lips, and life agree
To act a useful part.

When envy, strife, and wars begin
In little angry souls,
Mark how the sons of peace come in,
And quench the kindling coals.

Their minds are humble, mild and meek,
Nor let their fury rise;
Nor passion moves the lips to speak
Nor pride exalts their eyes.

Their frame is prudence mixed with love,
Good works fulfil their day;
They join the serpent with the dove,
But cast the sting away.

Such was the Savior of mankind,
Such pleasures he pursued;
His flesh and blood were all refined,
His soul divinely good.

Lord, can these plants of virtue grow
In such a heart as mine?
Thy grace my nature can renew,
And make my soul like thine.

Christ's Humiliation, Exaltation and Triumph

Phil. 2:8,9; Mark 15:20,24,29; Col. 2:15

Isaac Watts   J.L.Smith

The mighty frame of glorious grace,
That brightest monument of praise
That e'er the God of love designed,
Employs and fills my lab'ring mind.

Begin, my soul, the heav'nly song,
A burden for an angel's tongue:
When Gabriel sounds these awful things,
He tunes and summons all his stungs.

Proclaim inimitable love:
Jesus, the Lord of worlds above,
Puts off the beams of bright array,
And veils the God in mortal clay!

He that distributes crowns and thrones
Hangs on a tree, and bleeds, and groans!
The Prince of Life resigns his breath,
The King of Glory bows to death!

But see the wonders of his power,
He triumphs in his dying hour;
And while by Satan's rage he fell,
He dashed the rising hopes of hell.

Thus were the hosts of death subdued
And sin was drowned in Jesus' blood;
Thus he arose, and reigns above,
And conquers sinners by his love.

The Universal Law of Equity

Matt. 8:12

Isaac Watts

J.L. Smith

Blessed Redeemer, how divine,
How righteous is this rule of thine!
"To do to all men just the same
As we expect or wish from them."

This golden lesson, short and plain,
Gives not the mind nor mem'ry pain;
And every conscience must approve
This universal law of love.

How blest would every nation be,
Thus ruled by love and equity!
All would be friends without a foe,
And form a paradise below.

Jesus, forgive us, that we keep
Thy sacred law of love asleep;
No more let envy, wrath, and pride,
But thy blest maxims be our guide.

The Atonement of Christ

Rom. 3:25

Isaac Watts

J.L. Smith

How is our nature spoiled by sin!
Yet nature ne'er hath found
The way to make the conscience clean,
Or heal the painful wound.

In vain we seek for peace with God
By methods of our own:
Jesus, there's nothing but thy blood
Can bring us near the throne.

The threat'nings of thy broken law
Impress our souls with dread;
If God his sword of vengeance draw,
It strikes our spirits dead.

But thine illustrious sacrifice
Hath answered these demands:
And peace and pardon from the skies
Came down by Jesus' hands.

Here all the ancient types agree,
The altar and the lamb;
And prophets in their visions see
Salvation through his name.

'Tis by thy death we live, O Lord,
'Tis on thy cross we rest;
For ever be thy love adored,
Thy name for ever blessed.

The Business and Blessedness
of Glorified Saints

Rev. 7:13ff

Isaac Watts

J.L.Smith

"What happy men, or angels, these,
That all their robes are spotless white?
Whence did this glorious troop arrive
At the pure realms of heav'nly light?"

From torturing racks, and burning fires,
And seas of their own blood, they came;
But nobler blood has washed their robes,
Flowing from Christ the dying Lamb.

Now they approach th' Almighty throne
With loud hosannahs night and day;
Sweet anthems to the great Three One
Measure their blest eternity.

No more shall hunger pain their souls;
He bids their parching thirst begone,
And spreads the shadow of his wings
To screen them from the scorching sun.

The Lamb that fills the middle throne
Shall shed around his milder beams;
There shall they feast on his rich love,
And drink full joys from living streams.

Thus shall their mighty bliss renew
Through the vast round of endless years;
And the soft hand of sovereign grace
Heals all their wounds and wipes their tears.

Divine Wrath and Mercy

Nah. 1:1-3; Heb. 12:29

Isaac Watts

J.L.Smith

Adore and tremble, for our God
Is a consuming fire!
His jealous eyes his wrath inflame,
And raise his vengeance higher.

Almighty vengeance, how it burns!
How bright his fury glows!
Vast magazines of plagues and storms
Lie treasured for his foes.

Those heaps of wrath, by slow degrees,
Are forced into a flame;
But kindled, oh! how fierce they blaze!
And rend all nature's frame.

At his approach the mountains flee,
And seek a wat'ry grave;
The frighted sea makes haste away,
And shrinks up every wave.

Through the wide air the weighty rocks
Are swift as hailstones hurled;
Who dares engage his fiery rage
That shakes the solid world?

Yet, mighty God, thy sovereign grace
Sits regent on the throne;
The refuge of thy chosen race
When wrath comes rushing down.

Thy hand shall on rebellious kings
A fiery tempest pour,
While we beneath thy shelt'ring wings
Thy just revenge adore.

Jesus our Surety and Savior

1 Pet. 1:18; Gal. 3:13; Rom. 4:25

Isaac Watts

J.L.Smith

Adam, our father and our head,
Transgressed, and justice doomed us dead;
The fiery law speaks all despair:
There's no reprieve nor pardon there.

But, O unutterable grace
The Son of God takes Adam's place;
Down to our world the Savior flies,
Stretches his arms, and bleeds, and dies.

Justice was pleased to bruise the God,
And pay its wrongs with heav'nly blood:
What unknown racks and pangs he bore!
Then rose; the law could ask no more.

Amazing work! look down, ye skies,
Wonder and gaze with all your eyes;
Ye heav'nly thrones, stoop from above,
And bow to this mysterious love.

Lo! they adore th' incarnate Son,
And sing the glories he hath won;
Sing how he broke our iron chains,
How deep he suiik, how high he reigns!

Triumph and reign, victorious Lord,
By all the flaming hosts adored;
And say, dear Couqueror, say how long
Ere we shall rise to join their song.

Send down a chariot from above,
With fiery wheels, and paved with love
Raise us beyond th' ethereal blue,
To sing and love as angels do.

Christ's Dying, Rising and Reigning

Luke 23:27,29,44-46; Mt. 27:50,57; 28:6ff.

Isaac Watts

J.L.Smith

He dies! the friend of sinners dies!
Lo! Salem's daughters weep around;
A solemn darkness veils the skies;
A sudden trembling shakes the ground.

Come, saints, and drop a tear or two
For him who groaned beneath your load:
He shed a thousand drops for you,
A thousand drops of richer blood.

Here's love and grief beyond degree,
The Lord of glory dies for men!
But lo! what sudden joys we see;
Jesus the dead revives again!

The rising God forsakes the tomb!
The tomb in vain forbids his rise;
Cherubic legions guard him home,
And shout him welcome to the skies

Break off your fears, ye saints, and tell
How high our great Deliv'rer reigns;
Sing how he spoiled the hosts of hell,
And led the monster Death in chains.

Say, "Live for ever, wondrous King!
Born to redeem, and strong to save;
Then ask the monster, "Where's thy sting?"
And, "Where's thy vict'ry, boasting Grave?"

The Last Judgment
Rev. 21:5-8

Isaac Watts

J.L.Smith

See where the great incarnate God
Fills a majestic throne;
While from the skies his awful voice
Bears the last judgment down.

["I am the first, and I the last,
Through endless years the same;
I AM is my memorial still,
And my eternal name.

"Such favors as a God can give
My royal grace bestows:
Ye thirsty souls, come taste the streams,
Where life and pleasure flows.]

["The saint that triumphs o'er his sins,
I'll own him for a son;
The whole creation shall reward
The conquests he has won.

But bloody hands, and hearts unclean,
And all the lying race,
The faithless and the scoffing crew,
That spurn at offered grace;

"They shall be taken from my sight,
Bound fast in iron chains,
And headlong plunged into the lake
Where fire and darkness reigns."]

O may I stand before the Lamb,
When earth and seas are fled!
And hear the Judge pronounce my name,
With blessings on my head!

May I with those for ever dwell
Who here were my delight!
While sinners, banished down to hell,
No more offend my sight.

God Glorious and Sinners Saved

Rom. 1:30; 5:8,9; 1 Pet. 3:22

Isaac Watts

J.L. Smith

Father, how wide thy glories shine!
How high thy wonders rise!
Known through the earth by thousand signs,
By thousand through the skies.

Those mighty orbs proclaim thy power,
Their motions speak thy skill,
And on the wings of every hour
We read thy patience still.

But when we view thy strange design
To save rebellious worms,
Our souls are filled with awe divine
To see what God performs.

When sinners break the Father's laws,
The dying Son atones;
O the dear myst'ries of his cross,
The triumph of his groans

Now the full glories of the Lamb
Adorn the heav'nly plains;
Sweet cherubs learn Immanuel's name,
And try their choicest strains.

O may I bear some humble part
In that immortal song!
Wonder and joy shall tune my heart,
And love command my tongue.

The Works of Moses and the Lamb

Rev. 15:3

Isaac Watts

J.L.Smith

How strong thine arm is, mighty God!
Who would not fear thy name?
Jesus, how sweet thy graces are!
Who would not love the Lamb?

He has done more than Moses did,
Our Prophet and our King;
From bonds of hell he freed our souls,
And taught our lips to sing.

In the Red Sea, by Moses' hand,
Th' Egyptian host was drowned;
But his own blood hides all our sins
And guilt no more is found.

When through the desert Isr'el went,
With manna they were fed:
Our Lord invites us to his flesh,
And calls it living bread.

Moses beheld the promised land,
Yet never reached the place;
But Christ shall bring his followers home,
To see his Father's face.

Then shall our love and joy be full,
And feel a warmer flame;
And sweeter voices tune the song
Of Moses and the Lamb.

The Song of Zacharias

John 1:29, 32 Luke 1:68ff

Isaac Watts

J.L.Smith

Now be the God of Isr'el blessed,
Who makes his truth appear;
His mighty hand fulfils his word,
And all the oaths he sware.

Now he bedews old David's root
With blessings from the skies;
He makes the Branch of Promise grow,
The promised Horn arise.

[John was the prophet of the Lord,
To go before his face;
The herald which our Savior God
Sent to prepare his ways.

He makes the great salvation known,
He speaks of pardoned sins;
While grace divine, and heav'nly love,
In its own glory shines.

"Behold the Lamb of God," he cries.
"That takes our guilt away;
I saw the Spirit o'er his head,
On his baptizing day.]

Be every vale exalted high,
Sink every mountain low;
The proud must stoop, and humble souls
Shall his salvation know.

The heathen realms with Isr'el's land
Shall join in sweet accord
And all that's born of man shall see
The glory of the Lord.

Behold the Morning Star arise,
Ye that in darkness sit;
He marks the path that leads to peace,
And guides our doubtful feet."

Persevering Grace
Jude 1:24,25

J.L. Smith

Isaac Watts

To God the only wise,
Our Savior and our King,
Let all the saints below the skies
Their humble praises bring.

'Tis his almighty love,
His counsel, and' his care,
Preserves us safe from sin and death,
And every hurtful snare.

He will present our souls,
Unblemished and complete,
Before the glory of his face,
With joys divinely great.

Then all the chosen seed
Shall meet around the throne,
Shall bless the conduct of his
 grace,
And make his wonders known.

To our Redeemer, God,
Wisdom and power belongs,
Immortal crowns of majesty,
And everlasting songs.

Baptism

Acts 2:38; Matt. 28:19

Isaac Watts

J.L. Smith

'Twas the commission of our Lord,
"Go teach the nations, and baptize:"
The nations have received the word
Since he ascended to the skies.

He sits upon th' eternal hills,
With grace and pardon in his hands;
And sends his cov'nant with the seals,
To bless the distant British lands.

"Repent, and be baptized," he saith,
For the remission of your sins:"
And thus our sense assists our faith,
And shows us what his gospel means.

Our souls he washes in his blood,
As water makes the body clean;
And the good Spirit from our God
Descends like purifying rain.

Thus we engage ourselves to thee,
And seal our cov'nant with the Lord;
O may the great eternal Three
In heav'n our solemn vows record!

The Holy Scriptures

Heb. 1:1,2; 2 Tim. 3:15,16; Psa. 147:19,20

Isaac Watts

J.L.Smith

God, who in various methods told
His mind and will to saints of old,
Sent down his Son, with truth and grace,
To teach us in these latter days.

Our nation reads the written word,
That book of life, that sure record:
The bright inheritance of heav'n
Is by the sweet conveyance giv'n.

God's kindest thoughts are here expressed,
Able to make us wise and bless'd;
The doctrines are divinely true,
Fit for reproof and comfort too.

Ye British isles, who read his love
In long epistles from above,
(He hath not sent his sacred word
To every land,) praise ye the Lord.

Electing Grace

Eph. 1:3ff

Isaac Watts

J.L.Smith

Jesus, we bless thy Father's name;
Thy God and ours are both the same;
What heav'nly blessings from his throne
Flow down to sinners through his Son!

"Christ be my first elect," he said,
Then chose our souls in Christ our head,
Before he gave the mountains birth,
Or laid foundations for the earth.

Thus did eternal love begin
To raise us up from death and sin;
Our characters were then decreed,
"Blameless in love, a holy seed."

Predestinated to be sons,
Born by degrees, but chose at once,
A new regenerated race,
To praise the glory of his grace.

With Christ our Lord we share our part
In the affections of his heart;
Nor shall our souls be thence removed,
Till he forgets his first beloved.

Original Sin
Rom. 5:12; Psa. 51:5; Job 14:4

Isaac Watts

J.L.Smith

Backward with humble shame we look
On our original;
How is our nature dashed and broke
In our first father's fall!

To all that's good averse and blind,
But prone to all that's ill
What dreadful darkness veils our mind!
How obstinate our will!

[Conceived in sin, O wretched state!
Before we draw our breath
The first young pulse begins to beat
Iniquity and death.

How strong in our degen'rate blood
The old corruption reigns,
And, mingling with the crooked flood,
Wanders through all our veins.]

[Wild and unwholesome as the root
Will all the branches be;
How can we hope for living fruit
From such a deadly tree?

What mortal power from things unclean
Can pure productions bring?
Who can command a vital stream
From an infected spring?]

Yet, mighty God! thy wondrous love
Can make our nature clean,
While Christ and grace prevail above
The tempter, death, and sin.

The second Adam shall restore
The ruins of the first;
Hosannah to that sovereign power
That new-creates our dust!

Babylon Fallen

Rev. 18:20,21

Isaac Watts

J.L.Smith

In Gabriel's hand a mighty stone
Lies, a fair type of Babylon:
"Prophets, rejoice, and all ye saints,
God shall avenge your long complaints."

He said, and dreadful as he stood,
He sunk the millstone in the flood:
"Thus terribly shall Babel fall,
Thus, and no more be found at all."

The Virgin Mary's Song

Luke 2:46-55

Isaac Watts

J.L. Smith

"Our souls shall magnify the Lord,
In God the Savior we rejoice:
While we repeat the Virgin's song,
May the same Spirit tune our voice!

[The Highest saw her low estate,
And mighty things his hand hath done:
His overshadowing power and grace
Makes her the mother of his Son.

Let ev'ry nation call her blest,
And endless years prolong her fame;
But God alone must be ador'd:
Holy and reverend is his name.]

To those that fear and trust the Lord,
His mercy stands for ever sure:
From age to age his promise lives,
And the performance is secure.

He spake to Abram and his seed,
In thee shall all the earth be blessed;"
The memory of that ancient word
Lay long in his eternal breast.

But now no more shall Isr'el wait,
No more the Gentiles lie forlorn:
Lo, the desire of nations comes;
Behold, the promised seed is born!

Christ our High Priest and King

Rev. 1:5-7

Isaac Watts

J.L.Smith

Now to the Lord, that makes us know
The wonders of his dying love,
Be humble honors paid below,
And strains of nobler praise above.

'Twas he that cleansed our foulest sins,
And washed us in his richest blood;
'Tis he that makes us priests and kings,
And brings us rebels near to God.

To Jesus, our atoning Priest,
To Jesus, our superior King,
Be everlasting power confessed,
And every tongue his glory sing.

Behold, on flying clouds he comes,
And every eye shall see him move;
Though with our sins we pierced him once,
Then he displays his pard'ning love.

The unbelieving world shall wail,
While we rejoice to see the day:
Come, Lord; nor let thy promise fail,
Nor let thy chariots long delay.

Christ Jesus, the Lamb of God, Worshipped by all Creation
Rev. 5:11-13

Isaac Watts

J.L.Smith

Come, let us join our cheerful songs
With angels round the throne;
Ten thousand thousand are their tongues,
But all their joys are one.

"Worthy the Lamb that died," they cry,
"To be exalted thus:"
"Worthy the Lamb," our lips reply,
"For he was slain for us."

Jesus is worthy to receive
Honor and power divine;
And blessings more than we can give,
Be, Lord, for ever thine.

Let all that dwell above the sky,
And air, and earth, and seas,
Conspire to lift thy glories high,
And speak thine endless praise.

The whole creation join in one,
To bless the sacred name
Of him that sits upon the throne,
And to adore the Lamb.

Christ's Humiliation and Exaltation

Rev. 5:12

Isaac Watts

J.L.Smith

What equal honors shall we bring
To thee, O Lord our God, the Lamb,
When all the notes that angels sing
Are far inferior to thy name?

Worthy is he that once was slain,
The Prince of Peace that groaned and died;
Worthy to rise, and live, and reign
At his Almighty Father's side.

Power and dominion are his due
Who stood condemned at Pilate's bar;
Wisdom belongs to Jesus too,
Though he was charged with madness here.

All riches are his native right,
Yet he sustained amazing loss;
To him ascribe eternal might,
Who left his weakness on the cross.

Honor immortal must be paid,
Instead of scandal and of scorn;
While glory shines around his head,
And a bright crown without a thorn.

Blessings for ever on the Lamb
Who bore the curse for wretched men;
Let angels sound his sacred name,
And every creature say, Amen.

Adoption

1 John 3:1ff; Gal. 4:6

Isaac Watts

J.L.Smith

Behold what wondrous grace
The Father has bestowed
On sinners of a mortal race,
To call them sons of God!

'Tis no surprising thing
That we should be unknown;
The Jewish world knew not their king,
God's everlasting Son.

Nor doth it yet appear
How great we must be made;
But when we see our Savior here,
We shall be like our Head.

A hope so much divine
May trials well endure;
May purge our souls from sense and sin,
As Christ the Lord is pure.

If in my Father's love
I share a filial part,
Send down thy Spirit like a dove,
To rest upon my heart.

We would no longer lie
Like slaves beneath the throne;
My faith shall Abba, Father, cry,
And thou the kindred own.

The Day of Judgment

Rev. 11:15-18

Isaac Watts

J.L. Smith

Let the seventh angel sound on high,
Let shouts be heard through all the sky;
Kings of the earth, with glad accord,
Give up your kingdoms to the Lord.

Almighty God, thy power assume,
Who wast, and art, and art to come:
Jesus, the Lamb who once was slain,
For ever live, for ever reign!

The angry nations fret and roar,
That they can slay the saints no more
On wings of vengeance flies our God,
To pay the long arrears of blood.

Now must the rising dead appear;
Now the decisive sentence hear;
Now the dear martyrs of the Lord
Receive an infinite reward.

Justification by Faith, not by Works

Rom. 3:19-22

Isaac Watts

J.L. Smith

Vain are the hopes the sons of men
On their own works have built;
Their hearts by nature all unclean,
And all their actions guilt.

Let Jew and Gentile stop their mouths
Without a murm'ring word,
And the whole race of Adam stand
Guilty before the Lord.

In vain we ask God's righteous law
To justify us now;
Since to convince and to condemn
Is all the law can do.

Jesus, how glorious is thy grace!
When in thy name we trust,
Our faith receives a righteousness
That makes the sinner just.

Regeneration

John 1:13; 3:3

Isaac Watts   J.L. Smith

Not all the outward forms on earth,
Nor rites that God has giv'n,
Nor will of man, nor blood, nor birth,
Can raise a soul to heav'n.

The sovereign will of God alone
Creates us heirs of grace
Born in the image of his Son,
A new, peculiar race.

The Spirit, like some heav'nly wind,
Blows on the sons of flesh,
New-models all the carnal mind,
And forms the man afresh.

Our quickened souls awake, and rise
From the long sleep of death;
On heav'nly things we fix our eyes,
And praise employs our breath.

Election Excludes Boasting

1 Cor. 1:26-31

Isaac Watts

J.L. Smith

But few among the carnal wise,
But few of noble race,
Obtain the favor of thine eyes,
Almighty King of Grace.

He takes the men of meanest name
For sons and heirs of God;
And thus he pours abundant shame
On honorable blood.

He calls the fool, and makes him know
The myst'ries of his grace,
To bring aspiring wisdom low,
And all its pride abase.

Nature has all its glories lost
When brought before his throne;
No flesh shall in his presence boast,
But in the Lord alone.

Christ Our Wisdom

1 Cor. 1:30

Isaac Watts

J.L.Smith

Buried in shadows of the night
We lie till Christ restores the light;
Wisdom descends to heal the blind,
And chase the darkness of the mind.

Our guilty souls are drowned in tears
Till his atoning blood appears;
Then we awake from deep distress,
And sing, "The Lord our Righteousness."

Our very frame is mixed with sin,
His Spirit makes our natures clean
Such virtues from his suff'rings flow,
At once to cleanse and pardon too.

Jesus beholds where Satan reigns,
Binding his slaves in heavy chains;
He sets the pris'ners free, and breaks
The iron bondage from our necks.

Poor helpless worms in thee possess
Grace, wisdom, power, and righteousness;
Thou art our mighty All, and we
Give our whole selves, O Lord, to thee.

Victory Over Death

1 Cor. 15:55ff

Isaac Watts

J.L. Smith

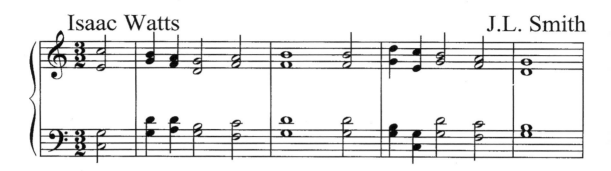

O for an overcoming faith
To cheer my dying hours;
To triumph o'er the monster Death,
And all his frightful powers!

Joyful with all the strength I have
My quiv'ring lips should sing-
Where is thy boasted vict'ry, Grave?
And where the monster's sting?

If sin be pardoned, I'm secure,
Death hath no sting beside;
The law gives sin its damning power;
But Christ, my ransom, died.

Now to the God of victory
Immortal thanks be paid,
Who makes us conquerors while we die,
Through Christ our living head.

Christ our Wisdom,
our Righteousness
1 Cor. 1:30

Isaac Watts

J.L.Smith

How heavy is the night
That hangs upon our eyes,
Till Christ with his reviving light
Over our souls arise!

Our guilty spirits dread
To meet the wrath of Heav'n;
But, in his righteousness arrayed,
We see our sins forgiv'n.

Unholy and impure
Are all our thoughts and ways;
His hands infected nature cure
With sanctifying grace.

The powers of hell agree
To hold our souls in vain;
He sets the sons of bondage free,
And breaks the cursed chain

Lord, we adore thy ways
To bring us near to God;
Thy sovereign power, thy healing grace,
And thine atoning blood.

Stone made Children of Abraham

Matt. 3:9

Isaac Watts

J.L. Smith

Vain are the hopes that rebels place
Upon their birth and blood,
Descended from a pious race;
Their fathers now with God.

He from the caves of earth and hell
Can take the hardest stones,
And fill the house of Abram well
With new-created sons.

Such wondrous power doth he possess
Who formed our mortal frame,
Who called the world from emptiness,
The world obeyed and came.

Believe and be Saved

John 3:16-18

Isaac Watts

J.L. Smith

Not to condemn the sons of men,
Did Christ, the Son of God, appear;
No weapons in his hands are seen,
No flaming sword nor thunder there.

Such was the pity of our God,
He loved the race of man so well,
He sent his Son to bear out load
Or sins, and saved our souls from hell.

Sinners, believe the Savour's word,
Trust in his mighty namd and live;
A thousand joys his lips afford,
His hands a thousand blessings give.

But vengeance and damnation lies
On rebels who refuse the grace;
Who God's eternal Son despise,
The hottest hell shall be their place.

Joy in Heaven for a Repenting Sinner

Luke 15:7, 10

Isaac Watts

J.L. Smith

Who can describe the joys that rise
Through all the courts of paradise,
To see a prodical return,
To see an heir of glory born?

With joy the Father doth approve
The fruit of his eternal love;
The Son with joy looks down and sees
The purchase of his agonies.

The Spirit takes delight in view
The holy soul he formed anew;
And saints and angels join to sing,
The growing empire of their King.

Not Ashamed of the Gospel

2 Tim. 1:12

Isaac Watts

J.L. Smith

I am not ashamed to own my Lord,
Or to defend his cause;
Maintain the honour of his word,
The glory of the cross.

Jesus, my God! I know his name,
His name is all my trust;
Nor will he put my soul to shame,
Nor let my hope be lost.

Firm as the throne he promise stands,
And he can well secure
What I've committed to his hands
Till the decisive hour.

Then will he own my worthless name
Before his Father's face,
And in the New Jerusalem
Appoint my soul a place.

The State and Nature of Grace

1 Cor. 6:10-11

Isaac Watts

J.L. Smith

Not the malicious or profane,
The wanton or the proud,
Nor thieves, nor sland'rers, shall obtain
The kingdom of our God.

Suprising grace! and such were we
By nature and by sin,
Heirs of immortal misery,
Unholy and unclean.

But we are washed in Jesus' blood,
We're pardoned through his name;
And the good Spirit of our God
Has sanctified our frame.

O for the persevering power
To keep thy just commands
We would defile our hearts no more,
No more pollute our hands.

Heaven Invisible and Holy

1 Cor. 2:9,10; Rev. 21:27

Isaac Watts

J.L.Smith

Nor eye hath seen, nor ear hath heard,
Nor sense nor reason known,
What joys the Father hath prepared
For those that love the Son.

But the good Spirit of the Lord
Reveals a heav'n to come;
The beams of glory in his word
Allure and guide us home.

Pure are the joys above the sky,
And all the region peace;
No wanton lips nor envious eye
Can see or taste the bliss.

Those holy gates for ever bar
Polution, sin, and shame
None shall obtain admittance there
But followers of the Lamb.

He keeps the Father's book of life,
There all their names are found;
The hypocrite in vain shall strive
To tread the heav'nly ground

Dead to Sin by the Cross of Christ

Rom. 6:1,2,6

Isaac Watts

J.L.Smith

Shall we go on to sin
Because thy grace abounds;
Or crucify the Lord again,
And open all his wounds?

Forbid it, mighty God!
Nor let it e'er be said,
That we whose sins are crucified
Should raise them from the dead.

We will be slaves no more,
Since Christ has made us free;
Has nailed our tyrants to the cross,
And bought our liberty.

Christ and Satan at Enmity

Gen. 3:1,15,17; Gal. 4:4; Col. 2:15

Isaac Watts

J.L.Smith

Deceived by subtle snares of hell,
Adam, our head, our father, fell;
When Satan, in the serpent hid,
Proposed the fruit that God forbid.

Death was the threat'ning: death began
To take possession of the man
His unborn race received the wound,
And heavy curses smote the ground.

But Satan found a worse reward;
Thus saith the vengeance of the Lord
"Let everlasting hatred be
Betwixt the woman's seed and thee.

"The woman's seed shall be my Son;
He shall destroy what thou hast done;
Shall break thy head, and only feel
Thy malice raging at his heel."

He spake; and bid four thousand years
Roll on; at length his Son appears;
Angels with joy descend to earth,
And sing the young Redeemer's birth.

Lo, by the sons of hell he dies;
But as he hung 'twixt earth and skies,
He gave their prince a fatal blow,
And triumph'd over the power below.

Christy Unseen and Beloved

1 Pet. 1:5

Isaac Watts

J.L. Smith

Now with our mortal eyes
Have we beheld the Lord;
Yet we rejoice to hear his name,
And love him in his word.

On earth we want the sight
Of our redeemer's face;
Yet, Lord, our inmost thoughts delight
To dwell upon thy grace.

And when we taste thy love,
Our joys divinely grow
Unspeakable, like those above,
And heav'n begins below.

The Value of Christ and His Righteousness

Phil. 3:7-9

Isaac Watts

J.L. Smith

No more, my God, I boast no more
Of all the duties I have done;
I quit the hope I held before,
To trust the merits of thy Son.

Now, for the love I bear his name,
What was my gain I count my loss;
My former pride I call my shame,
And nail my glory on the cross.

Yes, and I must and will esteem,
All things but loss for Jesus' sake;
O may my soul be found in him,
And of his righteousness partake!

The best obedience of my hands
Does not appear before thy throne;
But faith can answer thy demands
By pleading what my Lord has done.

Death and Immediate Glory

2 Cor. 5:1,5-8

Isaac Watts

J.L.Smith

There is a house not made with hands,
Eternal and on high;
And here my spirit waiting stands,
Till God shall bid it fly.

Shortly this prison of my clay
Must be dissolved and fall;
Then, O my soul! with joy obey
Thy heav'nly Father's call.

'Tis he, by his almighty grace,
That forms thee fit for heav'n;
And, as an earnest of the place,
Has his own Spirit giv'n.

We walk by faith of joys to come,
Faith lives upon his word;
But while the body is our home,
We're absent from the Lord.

'Tis pleasant to believe thy grace,
But we had rather see;
We would be absent from the flesh,
And present, Lord, with thee.

Salvation by Grace
Titus 3:3-7

Isaac Watts

J.L.Smith

[Lord, we confess our num'rous faults,
How great our guilt has been!
Foolish and vain were all our thoughts,
And all our lives were sin.

But, O my soul! for ever praise,
For ever love his name,
Who turns thy feet from dangerous ways
Of folly, sin, and shame.]

['Tis not by works of righteousness
Which our own hands have done;
But we are saved by sovereign grace
Abounding through his son.]

'Tis from the mercy of our God
That all our hopes begin;
'Tis by the water and the blood
Our souls are washed from sin.

'Tis through the purchase of his death
Who hung upon the tree,
The Spirit is sent down to breathe
On such dry bones as we.

Raised from the dead we live anew;
And, justified by grace,
We shall appear in glory too,
And see our Father's face.

The Brazen Serpent

John 3:14-16

Isaac Watts

J.L. Smith

So did the Hebrew prophet raise
The brazen serpent high,
The wounded felt immediate ease,
The camp forbore to die.

"Look upward in the dying hour,
And live," the prophet cries;
But Christ performs a nobler cure,
When Faith lifts up her eyes.

High on the cross the Savior hung,
High in the heav'ns he reigns:
Here sinners by th' old serpent stung
Look, and forget their pains.

When God's own Son is lifted up,
A dying world revives;
The Jew beholds the glorious hope,
Th' expiring Gentile lives.

Abraham's Blessing on the Gentiles

Gen. 17:7; Rom. 15:8; Mk 10:14

Isaac Watts

J.L.Smith

How large the promise, how divine,
To Abram and his seed!
"I'll be a God to thee and thine,
Supplying all their need."

The words of his extensive love
From age to age endure;
The Angel of the cov'nant proves,
And seals the blessing sure.

Jesus the ancient faith confirms,
To our great fathers giv'n;
He takes young children to his arms,
And calls them heirs of heav'n.

Our God, how faithful are his ways!
His love endures the same;
Nor from the promise of his grace
Blots out the children's name.

Abraham's Blessing on the Gentiles

Rom. 11:16-17

Isaac Watts

J.L.Smith

Gentiles by nature, we belong
To the wild olive wood;
Grace took us from the barren tree,
And grafts us in the good.

With the same blessings grace endows
The Gentile and the Jew;
If pure and holy be the root,
Such are the branches too.

Then let the children of the saints
Be dedicate to God,
Pour out thy Spirit on them, Lord,
And wash them in thy blood.

Thus to the parents and their seed
Shall thy salvation come,
And num'rous households meet at last
In one eternal home.

Conviction of Sin by the Law
Rom. 7:8,9,14,24

Isaac Watts

J.L.Smith

Lord, how secure my conscience was,
And felt no inward dread!
I was alive without the law,
And thought my sins were dead.

My hopes of heav'n were firm and bright,
But since the precept came
With a convincing power and light,
I find how vile I am.

[My guilt appeared but small before,
Till terribly I saw
How perfect, holy, just, and pure,
Was thine eternal law.

Then felt my soul the heavy load,
My sins revived again
I had provoked a dreadful God,
And all my hopes were slain.]

I'm like a helpless captive, sold
Under the power of sin
I cannot do the good I would,
Nor keep my conscience clean.

My God, I cry with every breath
For some kind power to save,
To break the yoke of sin and death,
And thus redeem the slave.

Love to God and Our God

Matt. 22:37-40

Isaac Watts

J.L. Smith

Thus saith the first, the great command,
"Let all thy inward powers unite
To love thy Maker and thy God
With utmost vigor and delight.

Then shall thy neighbor next in place
Share thine affections and esteem,
And let thy kindness to thyself
Measure and rule thy love to him."

This is the sense that Moses spoke,
This did the prophets preach and prove;
For want of this the law is broke,
And the whole law's fulfilled by love.

But O! how base our passions are!
How cold our charity and zeal!
Lord, fill our souls with heav'nly fire,
Or we shall ne'er perform thy will.

Election Sovereign and Free

Rom. 9:20-23

Isaac Watts

J.L. Smith

Behold the potter and the clay,
He forms his vessels as he please:
Such is our God, and such are we,
The subjects of his high decrees.

[Doth not the workman's power extend
O'er all the mass, which part to choose
And mold it for a nobler end,
And which to leave for viler use?]

May not the sovereign Lord on high
Dispense his favors as he will,
Choose some to life, while others die,
And yet be just and gracious still?

[What if, to make his terror known,
He lets his patience long endure,
Suff'ring vile rebels to go on,
And seal their own destruction sure?

What if he means to show his grace,
And his electing love employs
To mark out some of mortal race,
And form them fit for heav'nly joys?]

Shall man reply against the Lord,
And call his Maker's ways unjust,
The thunder of whose dreadful word
Can crush a thousand worlds to dust?

But, O my soul! if truths so bright
Should dazzle and confound thy sight,
Yet still his written will obey,
And wait the great decisive day.

Then shall he make his justice known,
And the whole world before his throne
With joy or terror shall confess
The glory of his righteousness.

Moses and Christ

John 1:17; Heb. 3:3,5,6; 10:28,29

Isaac Watts

J.L.Smith

The law by Moses came,
But peace, and truth, and love,
Were brought by Christ, a nobler name,
Descending from above.

Amidst the house of God
Their diff'rent works were done;
Moses a faithful servant stood,
But Christ a faithful Son.

Then to his new commands
Be strict obedience paid;
O'er all his Father's house he stands
The sovereign and the head.

The man that durst despise
The law that Moses brought,
Behold! how terribly he dies
For his presumptuous fault!

But sorer vengeance falls
On that rebellious race,
Who hate to hear when Jesus calls,
And dare resist his grace.

The Different Success of the Gospel

1 Cor. 1:23,24; 3:6,7; 2 Cor. 2:16

Isaac Watts

J.L.Smith

Christ and his cross is all our theme;
The myst'ries that we speak
Are scandal in the Jew's esteem,
And folly to the Greek.

But souls enlightened from above
With joy receive the word;
They see what wisdom, power, and love
Shine in their dying Lord.

The vital savor of his name
Restores their fainting breath;
But unbelief perverts the same
To guilt, despair, and death.

Till God diffuse his graces down,
Like showers of heav'nly rain,
In vain Apollos sows the ground,
And Paul may plant in vain.

Faith of Things Unseen
Heb. 11

Isaac Watts

J.L.Smith

Faith is the brightest evidence
Of things beyond our sight,
Breaks through the clouds of flesh and sense,
And dwells in heav'nly light.

It sets times past in present view,
Brings distant prospects home,
Of things a thousand years ago,
Or thousand years to come.

By faith we know the worlds were made
By God's almighty word;
Abram, to unknown countries led,
By faith obeyed the Lord.

He sought a city fair and high,
Built by th' eternal hands,
And faith assures us, though we die,
That heav'nly building stands.

Children Devoted to God

Gen. 17:7,10; Acts 16:14,15,33

Isaac Watts

J.L.Smith

Thus saith the mercy of the Lord,
"I'll be a God to thee;
I'll bless thy num'rous race, and they
Shall be a seed for me."

Abram believed the promised grace,
And gave his sons to God;
But water seals the blessing now,
That once was sealed with blood.

Thus Lydia sanctified her house,
When she received the word;
Thus the believing jailer gave
His household to the Lord.

Thus later saints, eternal King!
Thine ancient truth embrace;
To thee their infant offspring bring,
And humbly claim the grace.

79

Believers Buried with Christ in Baptism

Rom. 6:3, 4

Isaac Watts

J.L.Smith

Do we not know that solemn word,
That we are buried with the Lord,
Baptized into his death, and then
Put off the body of our sin?

Our souls receive diviner breath,
Raised from corruption, guilt, and death;
So from the grave did Christ arise,
And lives to God above the skies.

No more let sin or Satan reign
Over our mortal flesh again;
The various lusts we served before
Shall have dominion now no more.

The Repenting Prodigal
Luke 15:13-24

Isaac Watts

J.L.Smith

Behold the wretch whose lust and wine
Had wasted his estate,
He begs a share among the swine,
To taste the husks they eat!

"I die with hunger here," he cries,
"I starve in foreign lands;
My father's house has large supplies
And bounteous are his hands.

"I'll go, and with a mournful tongue
Fall down before his face,-
Father, I've done thy justice wrong,
Nor can deserve thy grace."

He ran, and fell upon his neck,
Embraced and kissed his son;
The rebel's heart with sorrow brake
For follies he had done.

"Take off his clothes of shame and sin,"
The father gives command,
"Dress him in garments white and clean,
With rings adorn his hand.

"A day of feasting I ordain,
Let mirth and joy abound;
My son was dead, and lives again,
Was lost, and now is found."

The First and Second Adam

Rom. 5:12

Isaac Watts

J.L. Smith

Deep in the dust before thy throne
Our guilt and our disgrace we own;
Great God! we own th' unhappy name
Whence sprang our nature and our shame;

Adam the sinner: at his fall,
Death like a conqueror seized us
A thousand new-born babes are dead
By fatal union to their head.

But whilst our spirits filled with awe,
Behold the terrors of thy law,
We sing the honors of thy grace,
That sent to save our ruined race.

We sing thine everlasting Son,
Who joined our nature to his own:
Adam the second from the dust
Raises the ruins of the first.

[By the rebellion of one man
Through all his seed the mischief ran;
And by one man's obedience now
Are all his seed made righteous too.]

Where sin did reign, and death abound,
There have the sons of Adam found
Abounding life; there glorious grace
Reigns through the Lord our righteousness.

Christ's compassion to the weak and tempted

Heb. 4:15,16; 5:7; Matt. 12:20

Isaac Watts

J.L.Smith

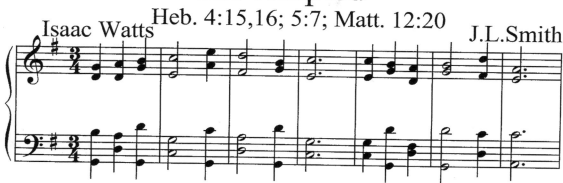

With joy we meditate the grace
Of our High Priest above;
His heart is made of tenderness,
His bowels melt with love.

Touched with a sympathy within,
He knows our feeble frame;
He knows what sore temptations mean,
For he has felt the same.

But spotless, innocent, and pure,
The great Redeemer stood,
While Satan's fiery darts he bore,
And did resist to blood.

He in the days of feeble flesh
Poured out his cries and tears,
And in his measure feels afresh
What every member bears.

[He'll never quench the smoking flax,
But raise it to a flame;
The bruised reed he never breaks,
Nor scorns the meanest name.]

Then let our humble faith address
His mercy and his power;
We shall obtain deliv'ring grace
In the distressing hour.

Charity and Uncharitableness

Rom. 14:17,19; 1 Cor. 10:32

Isaac Watts

J.L.Smith

Not diff'rent food, or diff'rent dress,
Compose the kingdom of our Lord;
But peace, and joy, and righteousness,
Faith, and obedience to his word.

When weaker Christians we despise,
We do the gospel mighty wrong;
For God, the gracious and the wise,
Receives the feeble with the strong.

Let pride and wrath be banished hence;
Meekness and love our souls pursue;
Nor shall our practice give offence
To saints, the Gentile or the Jew.

The Apostles' Commission

Mark 16:15ff, Matt. 28:18ff.

Isaac Watts

J.L. Smith

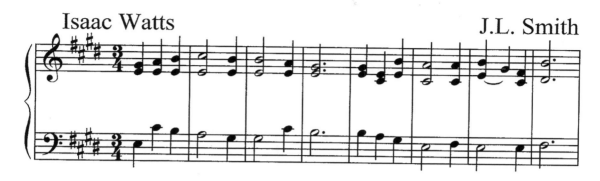

"O preach my gospel," saith the Lord,
"Bid the whole earth my grace receive;
He shall be saved that trusts my word,
He shall be damned that won't believe.

I'll make your great commission known,
And ye shall prove my gospel true,
By all the works that I have done,
By all the wonders ye shall do.

Go heal the sick, go raise the dead,
Go cast out devils in my name;
Nor let my prophets be afraid,
Though Greeks reproach, and Jews blaspheme.

Teach all the nations my commands
I'm with you till the world shall end;
All power is trusted to my hands,
I can destroy, and I defend."

He spake, and light shone round his head
On a bright cloud to heav'n he rode;
They to the farthest nations spread
The grace of their ascended God.

Love and Hatred

Phil. 2:2; Eph. 4:30

Isaac Watts

J.L.Smith

Now by the bowels of my God,
His sharp distress, his sore complaints,
By his last groans, his dying blood,
I charge my soul to love the saints.

Clamor, and wrath, and war, begone,
Envy and spite, for ever cease;
Let bitter words no more be known
Amongst the saints, the sons of peace.

The Spirit, like a peaceful dove,
Flies from the realms of noise and strife:
Why should we vex and grieve his love
Who seals our souls to heav'nly life?

Tender and kind be all our thoughts,
Through all our lives let mercy run;
So God forgives our num'rous faults,
For the dear sake of Christ his Son.

The Pharisee and the Publican
Luke 18:10-14

Isaac Watts

J.L. Smith

Behold how sinners disagree,
The publican and Pharisee!
One doth his righteousness proclaim,
The other owns his guilt and shame.

This man at humble distance stands,
And cries for grace with lifted hands
That boldly rises near the throne,
And talks of duties he has done.

The Lord their diff'rent language knows,
And diff'rent answers he bestows;
The humble soul with grace he crowns,
Whilst on the proud his anger frowns.

Dear Father! let me never be
Joined with the boasting Pharisee;
I have no merits of my own
But plead the suff'ring of thy Son.

Holiness and Grace

Titus 2:10-13

Isaac Watts

J.L.Smith

O let our lips and lives express
The holy gospel we profess;
So let our works and virtues shine,
To prove the doctrine all divine.

Thus shall we best proclaim abroad
The honors of our Savior God;
When the salvation reigns within,
And grace subdues the power of sin.

Our flesh and sense must be denied,
Passion and envy, lust and pride;
While justice, temp'rance, truth and love,
Our inward piety approve.

Religion bears our spirits up,
While we expect that blessed hope,
The bright appearance of the Lord,
And faith stands leaning on his word.

Love and Charity

1 Cor. 13:2-7, 13

Isaac Watts

J.L. Smith

Let Pharisees of high esteem
Their faith and zeal declare,
All their religion is a dream,
If love be wanting there.

Love suffers long with patient eye,
Nor is provoked in haste;
She lets the present injury die,
And long forgets the past.

Malice and rage, those fires of hell,
She quenches with her tongue;
Hopes and believes, and thinks no ill,
Though she endure the wrong.

She nor desires nor seeks to know
The scandals of the time;
Nor looks with pride on those below,
Nor envies those that climb.

She lays her own advantage by
To seek her neighbor's good;
So God's own Son came down to die,
And bought our lives with blood.

Love is the grace that keeps her power
In all the realms above;
There faith and hope are known no more,
But saints for ever love.

Religion Vain Without Love

1 Cor. 13:1-3

Isaac Watts

J.L.Smith

Had I the tongues of Greeks and Jews,
And nobler speech, that angels use,
If love be absent, I am found,
Like tinkling brass, an empty sound.

Were I inspired to preach and tell
All that is done in heav'n and hell;
Or could my faith the world remove,
Still I am nothing without love.

Should I distribute all my store
To feed the bowels of the poor,
Or give my body to the flame,
To gain a martyr's glorious name;

If love to God and love to men
Be absent, all my hopes are vain;
Nor tongues, nor gifts, nor fiery zeal,
The work of love can e'er fulfil.

The Love of Christ Shed Abroad in the Heart

Eph. 3:16ff

Isaac Watts

J.L.Smith

Come, dearest Lord, descend and dwell
By faith and love in every breast;
Then shall we know, and taste, and feel
The joys that cannot be expressed.

Come, fill our hearts with inward strength,
Make our enlarged souls possess,
And learn the height, and breadth, and length
Of thine unmeasurable grace.

Now to the God whose power can do
More than our thoughts or wishes know,
Be everlasting honors done
By all the church, through Christ his Son.

Sincerity and Hypocrisy

John 4:24; Ps. 139:23,24

Isaac Watts

J.L.Smith

God is a Spirit, just and wise,
He sees our inmost mind;
In vain to heav'n we raise our cries,
And leave our souls behind.

Nothing but truth before his throne
With honor can appear;
The painted hypocrites are known
Through the disguise they wear.

Their lifted eyes salute the skies,
Their bending knees the ground;
But God abhors the sacrifice,
Where not the heart is found.

Lord, search my thoughts, and try my ways,
And make my soul sincere
Then shall I stand before thy face,
And find acceptance there.

Salvation by Grace in Christ
2 Tim. 1:9,10

Isaac Watts

J.L.Smith

Now to the power of God supreme
Be everlasting honors giv'n;
He saves from hell, (we bless his name,)
He calls our wand'ring feet to heav'n.

Not for our duties or deserts,
But of his own abounding grace,
He works salvation in our hearts,
And forms a people for his praise.

'Twas his own purpose that begun
To rescue rebels doomed to die;
He gave us grace in Christ his Son
Before he spread the starry sky.

Jesus the Lord appears at last,
And makes his Father's counsels known;
Declares the great transactions past,
And brings immortal blessings down.

He dies, and in that dreadful night
Did all the powers of hell destroy;
Rising, he brought our heav'n to light,
And took possession of the joy.

Saints in the Hands of Christ

Jn. 10:28,29

Isaac Watts   J.L. Smith

Firm as the earth thy gospel stands,
My Lord, my hope, my trust;
If I am found in Jesus' hands,
My soul can ne'er be lost.

His honor is engaged to save
The meanest of his sheep;
All that his heav'nly Father gave
His hands securely keep.

Nor death nor hell shall e'er remove
His favorites from his breast;
In the dear bosom of his love
They must for ever rest.

The Witnessing and Sealing Spirit

Rom. 8:14,16; Eph. 1:13,14

Isaac Watts

J.L.Smith

Why should the children of a King
Go mourning all their days?
Great Comforter! descend and bring
Some tokens of thy grace.

Dost thou not dwell in all the saints,
And seal the heirs of heav'n?
When wilt thou banish my complaints,
And show my sins forgiv'n?

Assure my conscience of her part
In the Redeemer's blood
And bear thy witness with my heart,
That I am born of God.

Thou art the earnest of his love,
The pledge of joys to come;
And thy soft wings, celestial Dove,
Will safe convey me home.

Christ and Aaron
Heb. 7; 9

Isaac Watts

J.L.Smith

Jesus, in thee our eyes behold
A thousand glories more,
Than the rich gems and polished gold
The sons of Aaron wore.

They first their own burnt-offerings brought,
To purge themselves from sin;
Thy life was pure without a spot,
And all thy nature clean.

[Fresh blood as constant as the day
Was on their altar spilt;
But thy one offering takes away
For ever all our guilt.]

[Their priesthood ran through several hands,
For mortal was their race;
Thy never-changing office stands
Eternal as thy days.]

[Once in the circuit of a year,
With blood, but not his own,
Aaron within the veil appears
Before the golden throne:

But Christ, by his own powerful blood,
Ascends above the skies,
And in the presence of our God
Shows his own sacrifice.]

Jesus, the King of glory, reigns
On Zion's heav'nly hill;
Looks like a lamb that has been slain,
And wears his priesthood still.

He ever lives to intercede
Before his Father's face:
Give him, my soul, thy cause to plead,
Nor doubt the Father's grace.

Sinai and Zion

Heb. 12:18ff

Isaac Watts

J.L.Smith

Not to the terrors of the Lord,
The tempest, fire, and smoke;
Not to the thunder of that word
Which God on Sinai spoke;

But we are come to Zion's hill,
The city of our God,
Where milder words declare his will,
And spread his love abroad.

Behold th' innumerable host
Of angels clothed in light!
Behold the spirits of the just,
Whose faith is turned to sight!

Behold the blest assembly there
Whose names are writ in heav'n!
And God, the Judge of all, declares
Their vilest sins forgiv'n.

The saints on earth and all the dead
But one communion make;
All join in Christ their living Head,
And of his grace partake.

In such society as this
My weary soul would rest;
The man that dwells where Jesus is
Must be for ever blest.

With God is Terrible Majesty

Isaac Watts

J.L.Smith

Terrible God, that reign'st on high,
How awful is thy thund'ring hand!
Thy fiery bolts, how fierce they fly!
Nor can all earth or hell withstand.

This the old rebel angels knew,
And Satan fell beneath thy frown;
Thine arrows struck the traitor through,
And weighty vengeance sunk him down.

This Sodom felt, and feels it still,
And roars beneath th' eternal load:
"With endless burnings who can dwell?
Or bear the fury of a God?"

Tremble, ye sinners, and submit,
Throw down your arms before his throne;
Bend your heads low beneath his feet,
Or his strong hand shall crush you down.

And ye, blest saints, that love him too,
With rev'rence bow before his name;
Thus all his heav'nly servants do:
God is a bright and burning flame.

The Sight of God and Christ in Heaven

Isaac Watts

J.L. Smith

Descend from heav'n, immortal Dove,
Stoop down and take us on thy wings,
And mount and bear us far above
The reach of these inferior things:

Beyond, beyond this lower sky,
Up where eternal ages roll;
Where solid pleasures never die,
And fruits immortal feast the soul.

O for a sight, a pleasing sight
Of our Almighty Father's throne!
There sits our Savior crowned with light,
Clothed in a body like our own.

Adoring saints around him stand,
And thrones and powers before him fall;
The God shines gracious through the man,
And sheds sweet glories on them all.

O what amazing joys they feel
While to their golden harps they sing,
And sit on every heav'nly hill,
And spread the triumphs of their King!

When shall the day, dear Lord, appear,
That I shall mount to dwell above,
And stand and bow amongst them there,
And view thy face, and sing, and love?

Christ's Presence makes Death Easy

Isaac Watts

J.L.Smith

Why should we start, and fear to die
What timorous worms we mortals are!
Death is the gate of endless joy,
And yet we dread to enter there.

The pains, the groans, and dying strife,
Fright our approaching souls away;
Still we shrink back again to life,
Fond of our prison and our clay.

O! if my Lord would come and meet,
My soul should stretch her wings in haste,
Fly fearless through death's iron gate,
Nor feel the terrors as she passed.

Jesus can make a dying bed
Feel soft as downy pillows are,
While on his breast I lean my head,
And breathe my life out sweetly there.

Praise God for Creation
and Redemption

Isaac Watts

J.L. Smith

Let them neglect thy glory, Lord,
Who never knew thy grace;
But our loud songs shall still record
The wonders of thy praise.

We raise our shouts, O God, to thee,
And send them to thy throne;
All glory to th' united Three,
The undivided One.

'Twas he (and we'll adore his name)
That formed us by a word;
'Tis he restores our ruined frame:
Salvation to the Lord!

Hosannah! let the earth and skies
Repeat the joyful sound
Rocks, hills, and vales, reflect the voice
In one eternal round.

Christ's Intercession

Isaac Watts

J.L.Smith

Lift up your eyes to th' heav'nly seats
Where your Redeemer stays;
Kind Intercessor, there he sits,
And loves, and pleads, and prays.

'Twas well, my soul, he died for thee,
And shed his vital blood;
Appeased stern justice on the tree,
And then arose to God.

Petitions now, and praise may rise,
And saints their off'rings bring;
The Priest, with his own sacrifice,
Presents them to the King.

[Let papists trust what names they please,
Their saints and angels boast;
We've no such advocates as these,
Nor pray to th' heav'nly host.]

Jesus alone shall bear my cries
Up to his Father's throne;
He, dearest Lord! perfumes my sighs,
And sweetens every groan.

[Ten thousand praises to the King,
"Hosannah in the highest!"
Ten thousand thanks our spirits bring
To God and to his Christ.]

Love to God

Isaac Watts

J.L.Smith

Happy the heart where graces reign,
Where love inspires the breast;
Love is the brightest of the train,
And strengthens all the rest.

Knowledge, alas! 'tis all in vain,
And all in vain our fear;
Our stubborn sins will fight and reign,
If love be absent there.

'Tis love that makes our cheerful feet
In swift obedience move;
The devils know and tremble too,
But Satan cannot love.

This is the grace that lives and sings
When faith and hope shall cease;
'Tis this shall strike our joyful strings
In the sweet, realms of bliss.

Before we quite forsake our clay,
Or leave this dark abode,
The wings of love bear us away
To see our smiling God.

Christ's Sufferings and Glory

Isaac Watts

J.L.Smith

Now for a tune of lofty praise
To great Jehovah's equal Son!
Awake, my voice, in heav'nly lays
Tell the loud wonders he hath done.

Sing how he left the worlds of light,
And the bright robes he wore above;
How swift and joyful was his flight,
On wings of everlasting love!

[Down to this base, this sinful earth,
He came to raise our nature high;
He came t' atone Almighty wrath;
Jesus, the God, was born to die.]

[Hell and its lions roared around,
His precious blood the monsters spilt;
While weighty sorrows pressed him down,
Large as the loads of all our guilt.]

Deep in the shades of gloomy death
Th' almighty Captive pris'ner lay,
Th' almighty Captive left the earth,
And rose to everlasting day.

Lift up your eyes, ye sons of light,
Up to his throne of shining grace;
See what immortal glories sit
Round the sweet beauties of his face!

Amongst a thousand harps and songs,
Jesus, the God, exalted reigns;
His sacred name fills all their tongues,
And echoes through the heav'nly plains.

The Vengeance of God

Isaac Watts

J.L.Smith

With holy fear and humble song,
The dreadful God our souls adore;
Rev'rence and awe become the tongue
That speaks the terrors of his power.

Far in the deep where darkness dwells,
The land of horror and despair,
Justice has built a dismal hell,
And laid her stores of vengeance there.

[Eternal plagues, and heavy chains,
Tormenting racks, and fiery coals,
And darts t' inflict immortal pains,
Dyed in the blood of damned souls.]

[There Satan, the first sinner, lies,
And roars, and bites his iron bands;
In vain the rebel strives to rise,
Crushed with the weight of both thy hands.]

There guilty ghosts of Adam's race
Shriek out, and howl beneath thy rod
Once they could scorn a Savior's grace,
But they incensed a dreadful God.

Tremble, my soul, and kiss the Son;
Sinners, obey the Savior's call;
Else your damnation hastens on,
And hell gapes wide to wait your fall.

God's Condescension
to Human Affairs

Isaac Watts

J.L.Smith

Up to the Lord, that reigns on high,
And views the nations from afar,
Let everlasting praises fly,
And tell how large his bounties are.

[He that can shake the worlds he made,
Or with his word, or with his rod,
His goodness, how amazing great!
And what a condescending God!]

[God, that must stoop to view the skies,
And bow to see what angels do,
Down to our earth he casts his eyes,
And bends his footsteps downwards too.]

He overrules all mortal things,
And manages our mean affairs;
On humble souls the King of kings
Bestows his counsels and his cares.

Our sorrows and our tears we pour
Into the bosom of our God;
He hears us in the mournful hour,
And helps us bear the heavy load.

In vain might lofty princes try
Such condescension to perform;
For worms were never raised so high
Above their meanest fellow worm.

O could our thankful hearts devise
A tribute equal to thy grace,
To the third heav'n our songs should rise,
And teach the golden harps thy praise.

A Living and a Dead Faith

Isaac Watts

J.L.Smith

Mistaken souls, that dream of heav'n,
And make their empty boast
Of inward joys, and sins forgiv'n,
While they are slaves to lust!

Vain are our fancies, airy flights,
If faith be cold and dead;
None but a living power unites
To Christ the living head.

'Tis faith that changes all the heart;
'Tis faith that works by love;
That bids all sinful joys depart,
And lifts the thoughts above.

'Tis faith that conquers earth and hell
By a celestial power;
This is the grace that shall prevail
In the decisive hour.

[Faith must obey her Father's will,
As well as trust his grace;
A pard'ning God is jealous still
For his own holiness.]

When from the curse he sets us free,
He makes our natures clean;
Nor would he send his Son to be
The minister of sin.

[His Spirit purifies our frame,
And seals our peace with God;
Jesus and his salvation came
By water and by blood.]

Characteristics of the Children of God

Isaac Watts

J.L.Smith

So new-born babes desire the breast,
To feed, and grow, and thrive;
So saints with joy the gospel taste,
And by the gospel live.

[With inward gust their heart approves
All that the word relates;
They love the men their Father loves,
And hate the works he hates.]

[Not all the flatt'ring baits on earth
Can make them slaves to lust;
They can't forget their heav'nly birth,
Nor grovel in the dust.

Not all the chains that tyrants use
Shall bind their souls to vice;
Faith, like a conqueror, can produce
A thousand victories.]

They find access at every hour
To God within the veil;
Hence they derive a quick'ning power,
And joys that never fail.

O happy souls! O glorious state
Of overflowing grace!
To dwell so near their Father's seat,
And see his lovely face!

Lord, I address thy heav'nly throne;
Call me a child of thine;
Send down the Spirit of thy Son
To form my heart divine.

There shed thy choicest loves abroad,
And make my comforts strong:
Then shall I say, "My Father God!"
With an unwav'ring tougue.

Characteristics of Christ

Isaac Watts

J.L.Smith

Go, worship at Immanuel's feet,
See in his face what wonders meet!
Earth is too narrow to express
His worth, his glory, or his grace.

[The whole creation can afford
But some faint shadows of my Lord;
Nature, to make his beauties known,
Must mingle colors not her own.]

[Is he compared to wine or bread?
Dear Lord, our souls would thus be fed
That flesh, that dying blood of thine,
Is bread of life, is heav'nly wine.]

[Is he a tree? The world receives
Salvation from his healing leaves;
That righteous branch, that fruitful bough,
Is David's root and offspring too.]

[Is he a star? He breaks the night
Piercing the shades with dawning light;
I know his glories from afar,
I know the bright, the morning star.]

[Is he a sun? His beams are grace,
His course is joy and righteousness;
Nations rejoice when he appears
To chase their clouds and dry their tears.

O let me climb those higher skies,
Where storms and darkness never rise!
There he displays his power abroad,
And shines and reigns th' incarnate God.]

Nor earth, nor seas, nor sun, nor stars,
Nor heav'n, his full resemblance bears;
His beauties we can never trace,
Till we behold him face to face.

The Names and Titles of Christ

Isaac Watts

J.L.Smith

['Tis from the treasures of his word
I borrow titles for my Lord;
Nor art nor nature can supply
Sufficient forms of majesty.

Bright image of the Father's face,
Shining with undiminished rays;
Th' eternal God's eternal Son,
The heir and partner of his throne.]

The King of kings, the Lord most high,
Writes his own name upon his thigh
He wears a garment dipped in blood,
And breaks the nations with his rod.

Where grace can neither melt nor move,
The Lamb resents his injured love;
Awakes his wrath without delay,
And Judah's Lion tears the prey.

But when for works of peace he comes,
What winning titles he assumes!
Light of the world, and Life of men;
Nor bears those characters in vain.

With tender pity in his heart,
He acts the Mediator's part;
A Friend and Brother he appears,
And well fulfils the names he wears.

At length the Judge his throne ascends,
Divides the rebels from his friends,
And saints in full fruition prove
His rich variety of love.

The Offices of Christ

Isaac Watts

J.L.Smith

Join all the names of love and power
That ever men or angels bore,
All are too mean to speak his worth,
Or set Immannel's glory forth.

But O what condescending ways
He takes to teach his heav'nly grace
My eyes with joy and wonder see
What forms of love he bears for me.

[The Angel of the cov'nant stands
With his commission in his hands,
Sent from his Father's milder throne,
To make the great salvation known.]

[Great Prophet! let me bless thy name;
By thee the joyful tidings came
Of wrath appeased, of sins forgiv'n,
Of hell subdued, and peace with heav'n.]

[My Advocate appears on high,
The Father lays his thunder by;
Not all that earth or hell can say
Shall turn my Father's heart away.]

[My Lord, my Conqueror, and my King!
Thy sceptre and thy sword I sing;
Thine is the vict'ry, and I sit
A joyful subject at thy feet.]

[Aspire, my soul, to glorious deeds,
The Captain of salvation leads;
March on, nor fear to win the day,
Though death and hell obstruct the way.]

[Should death, and hell, and powers
    unknown,
Put all their forms of mischief on,
I shall be safe, for Christ displays
Salvation in more sovereign ways.

Prophecy and Inspiration

Isaac Watts

J.L.Smith

'Twas by an order from the Lord
The ancient prophets spoke his word;
His Spirit did their tongues inspire,
And warmed their hearts with heav'nly fire.

The works and wonders which they wrought
Confirmed the messages they brought;
The prophet's pen succeeds his breath,
To save the holy words from death.

Great God, mine eyes with pleasure look
On the dear volume of thy book;
There my Redeemer's face I see,
And read his name who died for me.

Let the false raptures of the mind
Be lost, and vanish in the wind;
Here I can fix my hope secure;
This is thy word, and must endure.

The Distemper, Folly and Madness of Sin

Isaac Watts

J.L. Smith

Sin, like a venomous disease,
Infects our vital blood;
The only balm is sovereign grace,
And the physician, God.

Our beauty and our strength are fled,
And we draw near to death;
But Christ the Lord recalls the dead
With his almighty breath.

Madness by nature reigns within,
The passions burn and rage,
Till God's own Son, with skill divine,
The inward fire assuage.

[We lick the dust, we grasp the wind,
And solid good despise;
Such is the folly of the mind,
Till Jesus makes us wise.

We give our souls the wounds they feel,
We drink the pois'nous gall,
And rush with fury down to hell;
But Heav'n prevents the fall.]

[The man possessed among the tombs
Cuts his own flesh, and cries;
He foams and raves, till Jesus comes,
And the foul spirit flies.]

Self-righteousness Insufficient

Isaac Watts   J.L.Smith

"Where are the mourners," saith the Lord,
"That wait and tremble at my word,
That walk in darkness all the day?
Come, make my name your trust and stay.

["No works nor duties of your own
Can for the smallest sin atone
The robes that nature may provide
Will not your least pollutions hide.

"The softest couch that nature knows
Can give the conscience no repose;
Look to my righteousness and live;
Comfort and peace are mine to give.]

"Ye sons of pride, that kindle coals
With your own hands, to warm your souls
Walk in the light of your own fire,
Enjoy the sparks that ye desire:

"This is your portion at my hands;--
Hell waits you with her iron bands;
Ye shall lie down in sorrow there,
In death, in darkness, and despair."

Christ our Passover

Isaac Watts

J.L.Smith

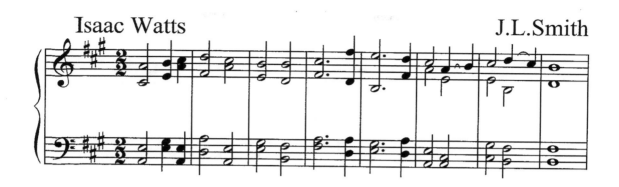

Lo, the destroying angel flies
To Pharaoh's stubborn land;
The pride and flower of Egypt dies
By his vindictive hand.

He passed the tents of Jacob o'er,
Nor poured the wrath divine;
He saw the blood on every door,
And blessed the peaceful sign.

Thus the appointed Lamb must bleed,
To break the Egyptian yoke;
Thus Isr'el is from bondage freed,
And 'scapes the angel's stroke.

Lord, if my heart were sprinkled too
With blood so rich as thine,
Justice no longer would pursue
This guilty soul of mine.

Jesus our passover was slain,
And has at once procured
Freedom from Satan's heavy chain,
And God's avenging sword.

Presumption and Despair

Isaac Watts

J.L.Smith

I hate the tempter and his charms,
I hate his flatt'ring breath;
The serpent takes a thousand forms
To cheat our souls to death.

He feeds our hopes with airy dreams,
Or kills with slavish fear;
And holds us still in wide extremes,
Presumption or despair.

Now he persuades, "How easy 'tis
To walk the road to heav'n;"
Anon he swells our sins, and cries,
"They cannot be forgiv'n."

[He bids young sinners "yet forbear
To think of God, or death;
For prayer and devotion are
But melancholy breath.

He tells the aged, "they must die,
"And 'tis too late to pray;
In vain for mercy now they cry,
For they have lost their day."]

Thus he supports his cruel throne
By mischief and deceit,
And drags the sons of Adam down
To darkness and the pit.

Almighty God, cut short his power,
Let him in darkness dwell
And that he vex the earth no more,
Confine him down to hell.

116

Satan's Devices

Isaac Watts

J.L.Smith

Now Satan comes with dreadful roar
And threatens to destroy;
He worries whom he can't devour
With a malicious joy.

Ye sons of God, oppose his rage,
Resist, and he'll begone;
Thus did our dearest Lord engage
And vanquish him alone.

Now he appears almost divine,
Like innocence and love;
But the old serpent lurks within
When he assumes the dove.

Fly from the false deceiver's tongue,
Ye sons of Adam, fly;
Our parents found the snare too strong,
Nor should the children try.

The Almost Christian

Isaac Watts

J.L.Smith

Broad is the road that leads to death,
And thousands walk together there;
But wisdom shows a narrower path,
With here and there a traveller.

"Deny thyself, and take thy cross,"
Is the Redeemer's great command;
Nature must count her gold but dross,
If she would gain this heav'nly land.

The fearful soul that tires and faints,
And walks the ways of God no more,
Is but esteemed almost a saint,
And makes his own destruction sure.

Lord, let not all my hopes be vain
Create my heart entirely new;
Which hypocrites could ne'er attain,
Which false apostates never knew.

Converting Grace

Isaac Watts

J.L.Smith

[Great King of glory and of grace,
We own, with humble shame,
How vile is our degen'rate race,
And our first father's name.]

From Adam flows our tainted blood,
The poison reigns within;
Makes us averse to all that's good,
And willing slaves to sin.

[Daily we break thy holy laws,
And then reject thy grace;
Engaged in the old serpent's cause,
Against our Maker's face.]

We live estranged afar from God,
And love the distance well;
With haste we run the dangerous road
That leads to death and hell.

And can such rebels be restored?
Such natures made divine?
Let sinners see thy glory, Lord,
And feel this power of thine.

We raise our Fathers name on high
Who his own Spirit sends
To bring rebellious strangers nigh,
And turn his foes to friends.

Custom in Sin

Isaac Watts

J.L.Smith

Let the wild leopards of the wood
Put off the spots that nature gives,
Then may the wicked turn to God,
And change their tempers and their lives.

As well might Ethiopian slaves
Wash out the darkness of their skin,
The deed as well might leave their graves,
As old transgressors cease to sin.

Where vice has held its empire long,
'Twill not endure the least control;
None but a power divinely strong
Can turn the current of the soul.

Great God! I own thy power divine
That works to change this heart of mine;
I would be formed anew, and bless
The wonders of creating grace.

Christian Virtues

Isaac Watts

J.L.Smith

Strait is the way, the door is strait,
That leads to joys on high;
'Tis but a few that find the gate,
While crowds mistake, and die.

Beloved self must be denied,
The mind and will renewed
Passion suppressed, and patience tried,
And vain desires subdued.

[Flesh is a dangerous foe to grace,
Where it prevails and rules;
Flesh must be humbled, pride abased,
Lest they destroy our souls.

The love of gold be banished hence,
That vile idolatry,
And every member, every sense,
in sweet subjection lie.]

The tongue, that most unruly power,
Requires a strong restraint;
We must be watchful every hour,
And pray, but never faint.

Lord, can a feeble, helpless worm
Fulfil a task so hard?
Thy grace must all my work perform,
And give the free reward.

The Joy of Faith

Isaac Watts

J.L.Smith

My thoughts surmount these lower skies,
And look within the veil;
There springs of endless pleasure rise,
The waters never fail.

There I behold, with sweet delight,
The blessed Three in One;
And strong affections fix my sight
On God's incarnate Son.

His promise stands for ever firm,
His grace shall ne'er depart;
He binds my name upon his arm,
It seals on his heart.

Light are the pains that nature brings;
How short our sorrows are,
When with eternal future things
The present we compare!

I would not be a stranger still
To that celestial place,
Where I for ever hope to dwell
Near my redeemer's face.

Complaint of Desertion
and Temptations

Isaac Watts

J.L. Smith

Dear Lord! behold our sore distress;
Our sins attempt to reign;
Stretch out thine arm of conquering grace,
And let thy foes be slain.

[The lion with his dreadful roar
Affrights thy feeble sheep:
Reveal the glory of thy power,
And chain him to the deep.

Must we indulge a long despair?
Shall our petitions die?
Our mourning's never reach thine ear,
Nor tears affect thine eye?]

If thou despise a mortal groan,
Yet hear a Savior's blood;
An Advocate so near the throne
Pleads and prevails with God.

He brought the Spirit's powerful sword
To slay our deadly foes;
Our sins shall die beneath thy word,
And hell in vain oppose.

How boundless is our Father's grace,
In height, and depth, and length!
He makes his Son our righteousness,
His Spirit is our strength.

The End of the World

Isaac Watts

J.L.Smith

Why should this earth delight us so?
Why should we fix our eyes
On these low grounds where sorrows grow,
And every pleasure dies ?

While time his sharpest teeth prepares
Our comforts to devour,
There is a land above the stars,
And joys above his power.

Nature shall be dissolved and die,
The sun must end his race,
The earth and sea for ever fly
Before my Savior's face.

When will that glorious morning rise?
When the last trumpet sound,
And call the nations to the skies,
From underneath the ground?

Unfruitfulness, Ignorance and Unsanctified affections

Isaac Watts

J.L.Smith

Long have I sat beneath the sound
Of thy salvation, Lord;
But still how weak my faith is found,
And knowledge of thy word!

Oft I frequent thy holy place,
And hear almost in vain;
How small a portion of thy grace
My memory can retain!

[My dear Almighty, and my God,
How little art thou known
By all the judgments of thy rod,
And blessings of thy throne!]

How cold and feeble is my love!
How negligent my fear!
How low my hope of joys above!
How few affections there!

Great God! thy sovereign power impart
To give thy word success;
Write thy salvation in my heart,
And make me learn thy grace.

[Show my forgetful feet the way
That leads to joys on high;
There knowledge grows without decay,
And love shall never die.]

The Divine Perfections

Isaac Watts

J.L.Smith

How shall I praise th' eternal God,
That infinite Unknown?
Who can ascend his high abode,
Or venture near his throne?

[The great Invisible! he dwells
Concealed in dazzling light;
But his all-searching eye reveals
The secrets of the night.

Those watchful eyes that never sleep
Survey the world around
His wisdom is a boundless deep
Where all our thoughts are drowned.]

[Speak we of strength? his arm is strong
To save or to destroy;
Infinite years his life prolong,
And endless is his joy.]

[He knows no shadow of a change
Nor alters his decrees;
Firm as a rock his truth remains
To guard his promises.]

[Sinners before his presence die;
How holy is his name!
His anger and his jealousy
Burn like devouring flame.]

Justice upon a dreadful throne
Maintains the rights of God;
While Mercy sends her pardons down,
Bought with a Savior's blood.

Now to my soul, immortal King!
Speak some forgiving word;
Then 'twill be double joy to sing
The glories of my Lord.

The Divine Perfections

Isaac Watts

J.L. Smith

Great God! thy glories shall employ
My holy fear, my humble joy;
My lips in songs of honor bring
Their tribute to th' eternal King.

[Earth, and the stars, and worlds unknown,
Depend precarious on his throne;
All nature hangs upon his word,
And grace and glory own their Lord.]

[His sovereign power what mortal knows?
If be command, who dares oppose?
With strength he girds himself around,
And treads the rebels to the ground.]

[Who shall pretend to teach him skill,
Or guide the counsels of his will?
His wisdom, like a sea divine,
Flows deep and high beyond our line.]

[Th' eternal law before him stands;
His justice, with impartial hands,
Divides to all their due reward,
Or by the sceptre or the sword.]

[His mercy, like a boundless sea,
Washes our load of guilt away;
While his own Son came down and died
T' engage his justice on our side.]

[Each of his words demands my faith;
My soul can rest on all he saith;
His truth inviolably keeps
The largest promise of his lips.]

O tell me, with a gentle voice,
"Thou art my God," and I'll rejoice!
Filled with thy love, I dare proclaim
The brightest honours of the name.

The Divine Perfections

Isaac Watts

J.L.Smith

Jehovah reigns, his throne is high,
His robes are light and majesty;
His glory shines with beams so bright,
No mortal can sustain the sight.

His terrors keep the world in awe;
His justice guards his holy law;
His love reveals a smiling face;
His truth and promise seal the grace.

Through all his works his wisdom shines,
And baffles Satan's deep designs;
His power is sovereign to fulfil
The noblest counsels of his will.

And will this glorious Lord descend
To be my Father and my Friend?
Then let my songs with angels join;
Heav'n is secure, if God be mine.

God Incomprehensible and Sovereign

Isaac Watts

J.L.Smith

[Can creatures to perfection find
Th' eternal, uncreated Mind?
Or can the largest stretch of thought
Measure and search his nature out?

'Tis high as heav'n, 'tis deep as hell
And what can mortals know or tell?
His glory spreads beyond the sky,
And all the shining worlds on high.

But man, vain man, would fain be wise;
Born like a wild young colt, he flies
Through all the follies of his mind,
And swells, and snuffs the empty wind.]

God is a King of power unknown,
Firm are the orders of his throne;
If he resolve, who dares oppose,
Or ask him why or what he does.

He wounds the heart, and he makes whole
He calms the tempest of the soul;
When he shuts up in long despair,
Who can remove the heavy bar?

He frowns, and darkness veils the moon;
The fainting sun grows dim at noon;
The pillars of heav'n's starry roof
Tremble and start at his reproof.

He gave the vaulted heav'n its form,
The crooked serpent, and the worm;
He breaks the billows with his breath,
And smites the sons of pride to death.

These are a portion of his ways;
But who shall dare describe his face?
Who can endure his light, or stand
To hear the thunders of his hand?

Meter Index

Scripture Index

Hymn Index